From Your Friends At **The MAILBOX®**

Busy Kids™
CENTERS

Written by:
Jan Brennan
Ann Flagg
Lisa Leonardi
Dayle Timmons

Edited by:
Ada Goren
Mackie Rhodes

Illustrated by:
Susan Hodnett
Rebecca Saunders

Cover designed by:
Kimberly Richard

The Education Center®

Manufactured in the United States
10 9 8 7 6 5 4 3 2 1

Busy Kids™
Centers

Table Of Contents

Introduction

Does planning activities for your center time seem like a three-ring circus? Then step right up! *Busy Kids™: Centers* provides ideas for enhancing traditional centers and for creating easy-to-set-up thematic centers. These ideas—centered around more than 25 popular early-childhood themes—reinforce skills and thematic instruction, and provide fun learning opportunities for children with different learning styles. With all it has to offer, you're sure to find this book a real crowd pleaser!

Focus Your Attention On The Center Ring:

- **Provide a combination of both quiet and active centers.** Otherwise you'll have to tame the crowd!

- **Continue center activities** for the duration of your theme—or longer if your audience is truly captivated!

- **Avoid doing a juggling act.** Make most of your centers independent rather than teacher-directed.

- **Encourage free exploration** in your center activities. Take a break from your duties as ringmaster and allow youngsters to run the show.

- **Be versatile.** Give youngsters a variety of attractions to experience.

- **Take a front-row seat.** You'll be amazed at what you can learn about your youngsters as you observe their center play.

BUNNIES AND BASKETS

BUNCHES OF BUNNIES

"Hare's" an activity to get your little bunnies hoppin' to the art center to create their own bunnies. To prepare, supply the center with white paper doilies of two sizes, construction paper, a tagboard bunny-ear pattern, pink paper, pompoms, sticky dots, and short lengths of pipe cleaners. To create a bunny, a child glues a small and a large doily to a sheet of construction paper to form a bunny's head and body. He traces the ear pattern twice onto pink paper, then cuts out the ears and glues them to the bunny's head. He then attaches a pom-pom nose, two sticky-dot eyes, and pipe-cleaner whiskers to complete his bunny. This center is sure to be "rabbit-forming!"

SAND-FILLED EGGS

Your youngsters will get their fill of this "egg-citing" sand-table activity. Place a supply of colored plastic eggs in the sand table. Add plastic baskets for collecting eggs. Invite each student to fill some egg halves with sand, fit each with its corresponding half, and then collect the eggs in his basket. After all the eggs have been collected, ask youngsters to empty the contents of their eggs back into the sand table for the next group of bunnies. At a later time, you might have youngsters fill the eggs with toy critters, such as snakes, turtles, chicks, or other egg-hatching animals. Time to get cracking!

SEQUENCING STICKS

Challenge youngsters' sequencing skills with this math-center activity. To prepare, gather several sets of ten wide craft sticks and an assortment of ministickers, such as rabbits, eggs, and flowers. On each stick in a set, adhere a different number of identical stickers from one to ten. To prevent the stickers from peeling off, paint each stick with clear fingernail polish and let it dry. Then place each set of sticks in a separate basket. To use, invite student pairs to sequence the sticks in each set. Further challenge them to group together the sticks from each set having the same number of stickers. Then have the children return the stick sets to the baskets for the next pair.

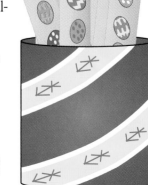

WONDERFUL WEAVES

Have your little hares hop over to the paint easel for a basketful of weaving fun. To prepare, cut a class supply of large construction-paper baskets. Then enlist the help of your little ones to tear different colors of construction paper into strips. Put the paper strips in a basket near the easel. Fill a paint pot with glue and add a paintbrush. Then clip a basket cutout to the easel. Show each little artist how to paint the cutout with glue and then add colorful strips of construction paper to create a basket weave. After the baskets are dry, have youngsters trim the excess paper from the basket edges. What wonderful weaves!

BUNNY BOX

Outfit youngsters with this prop-filled bunny box for some rabbit role-playing fun. In advance, collect bunny ears, baskets, a fancy hat, a bow tie or vest, and colored plastic eggs. Place the items in a cardboard box covered with Easter gift wrap; then put the box in your dramatic-play center. Invite youngsters to use the contents of the box as they role-play rabbit themes and schemes. Soon your little bunnies will be acting out their own "hoppily-ever-after" stories!

Christmas

Season's Readings

Book time for plenty of Christmas reading this season. After reading an assortment of Christmas books to your little ones, display three of the books on a table in your reading center. Ask each child to illustrate the Christmas story he most enjoyed. Label his drawing with the title of the book. Then display each child's illustration with the corresponding title. Which book is the class favorite? Whatever the results, season's readings abound!

Stocking Sense

Heighten the senses of the season at your discovery center. To prepare, wrap three small items in holiday gift wrap and place them inside a large Christmas stocking. On a sheet of chart paper, draw the three items along with three more items that are not inside the stocking; then hang the chart paper near the stocking.

Ask each child who visits this center to use her senses of touch, sight, hearing, and even smell to guess what the three objects are. Have her indicate her guess by putting a check beside the drawings that represent her guesses. At the end of the day, discuss the children's guesses; then unwrap the three packages for all to see. Repeat the activity on another day by wrapping three different items to put inside the stocking.

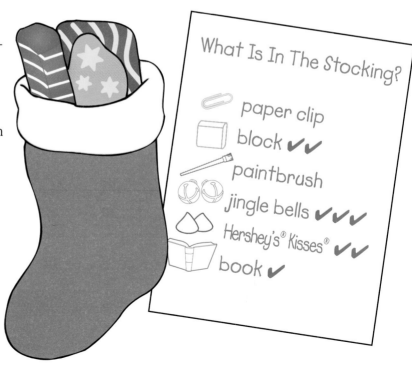

What Is In The Stocking?

paper clip
block ✔✔
paintbrush
jingle bells ✔✔✔
Hershey's® Kisses® ✔✔
book ✔

Seasonal Gift Wrap

Wrap up the Christmas season with this art-center activity. Stock your art center with a variety of Christmas cookie cutters, 12-inch lengths of white bulletin-board paper (one for each child), and shallow trays of red and green tempera paint. Invite the children to make cookie-cutter prints on their papers. Encourage them to experiment with various designs, colors, and patterns as they work. After the paint dries, allow each student to use her decorated paper to wrap a special gift for a special someone.

Ornamental Math

Shape up your math table for the holidays with this festive sorting activity. In advance, send each child home with a note requesting that he bring an unbreakable Christmas ornament to school. Then cut out one small, one medium, and one large construction-paper circle. Place a small artificial tree and the cutouts in the math center. As children bring their ornaments to school, have them hang their decorations on the tree. When the tree is fully decorated, encourage small groups of youngsters to remove the ornaments and place each one on the construction-paper circle corresponding to its size (small, medium, or large). After all the ornaments have been sorted, invite your little elves to trim the tree all over again!

Santa Station

Convert your dramatic-play center into a Santa station. Gather items to create a Santa costume, such as a Santa hat, a white beard, an oversized red shirt, black boots, and a large sack (or a pillowcase). Collect more Santa hats and long red shirts to serve as elf costumes. Wrap several small boxes or cardboard blocks in holiday paper; then place them in the center along with the Santa props and a tape recording of holiday music. Hang several stockings on a wall or table in the center. Then invite youngsters to use the props to role-play Santa and his elves preparing for the big event. Ho! Ho! Ho!

susan Hodnett

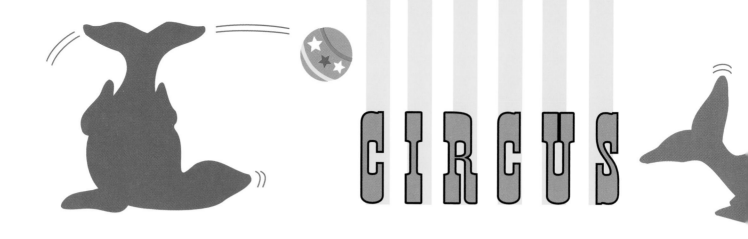

CIRCUS

The Circus Train

Your youngsters will want to hop aboard this circus train activity! To prepare, gather a class supply of cereal or cracker boxes, some toy circus animals, and several pipe cleaners. Trim each box to about three inches high. Punch a hole in the short sides of each box. Then cut train wheels from black construction paper.

Have each child paint a box with a color of his choice. When the boxes are dry, have him glue construction-paper wheels to his box train car. To assemble the cars into a train, have youngsters connect them with pipe-cleaner halves. Finally, invite the children to load up the train with animals, then chug on over to the dramatic-play center or the block center for some imaginative play.

Hoops And Scoops

It's time for some new tricks at an old favorite—the water table. Collect a few small balls that float, such as Ping-Pong® balls or rubber bouncy balls. Then head to the party-supply store for some inexpensive plastic ring bracelets. Float the bracelets in the water and encourage your young circus performers to drop balls into the hoops from different levels. Add scoops and cups to the bracelets and balls, and your little ones will no doubt invent some new tricks of their own!

Under The Big Top

Turn your block area into an amazing three-ring circus. Put three plastic hoops on the floor of the block area to define workspaces. Gather toys and other items to represent circus characters and props, such as toy animals and people, dollhouse chairs, and ring bracelets. Present these items to the class, encouraging the children to brainstorm how these and other things in the room might be used to create imaginary circus acts. For example, the chairs might be used as lion-taming tools, while the bracelets might serve as jumping hoops for circus dogs. Then place the circus props in the block area. Assign one child at a time to each plastic hoop; then invite him to create a circus act inside his "ring." If desired, take instant photos of each act. Display the photographs in the block area to ignite the imaginations of the rest of your little ringmasters.

Estimation Sensation

Youngsters will be more than willing to pop into your sensory center for this estimating activity. Send each child home with a note requesting that each family send in a bag of cooked popcorn. Empty the bags into your sensory table; then add scoops and some paper lunch bags. Explain to youngsters that this popcorn is to play with—not to eat! Then have visitors to the center estimate the number of popcorn scoops needed to fill a bag. Invite each child to count the actual number of scoops needed, then compare that amount with her estimate. After all your little ones have enjoyed this circus attraction, scatter the popcorn outdoors as a treat for the birds. Then serve youngsters a freshly popped batch of popcorn at snacktime.

Clown "Mask-erades"

Send your little ones to the art center to make funny masks for clowning around. In advance, inflate and knot a class supply of small, round balloons. Then prepare a mask for each child by cutting two eyeholes and a nosehole in a paper plate. Staple a craft stick to the plate to serve as a handle. Place the balloons, masks, and an assortment of construction-paper shapes in the art center. Encourage each child to create a clown mask by gluing paper-shape features—such as ears, hair, and accessories—onto the plate. Then help her attach a silly balloon nose to her mask by pulling the knotted end of a balloon through the nosehole and securing it with tape. Invite your little clowns to don their silly masks for a few laughs in your dramatic-play center.

Note: Balloons can be a choking hazard for small children. Provide close supervision.

Caroline wants to be a nurse when she grows up so she can help sick people get better.

Future Careers

What does the future hold for each of your students? Invite them to share their vision at the art center! In advance, gather lots of images of working people—from magazine pictures, books, or clip art; then put these in a basket in your art center. Invite each child who visits the center to browse through the pictures, then select one that she envisions for herself. Encourage her to draw a picture of herself as her chosen worker. Write each child's dictation about her career on her paper. Display the drawings in your classroom.

Letter-Perfect Career Choices

Encourage your little ones to spell out their career choices with this tip-top center activity. To prepare, gather a collection of dress-up hats or ask parents to donate or lend hats associated with various careers. Display the hats near a full-length mirror in your dramatic-play center. Invite youngsters to don the different hats; then take an instant photo of each child in the hat of his choice. In the space below the photo, use a permanent marker to write the occupation associated with the hat. Then place the photos, a cookie sheet, and a basket of magnetic letters in a center. Challenge students to use the letters to spell out the occupations written on the photos.

FIREFIGHTER

FIREFI

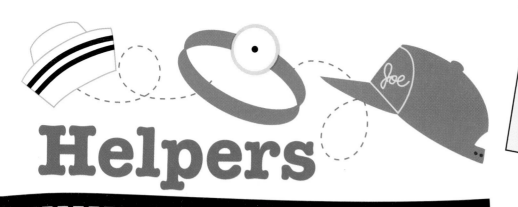

Helpers

Tool Time

Set up a building center for your budding architects and carpenters. To begin, gather a supply of golf tees, wooden blocks, plastic knives, and large pieces of Styrofoam® packaging to place in a center. Then invite your builders to create structures using the Styrofoam® building material, wooden-block hammers, golf-tee nails, and plastic-knife saws. Just watch the enthusiasm build at this center designed for fun!

Career Categories

Set up a center to expose your students to all sorts of jobs. Cut out magazine and catalog pictures representing workers, tools, and clothing associated with different jobs. Glue each cutout onto a separate tagboard card. Put the cards in a center; then encourage each little worker to sort the cards according to the related jobs. For an added challenge, have the child sort the cards into three groups— workers, tools, and career clothing. Then compliment the child on a job well done!

Construction Zone

Are there some future construction workers in your group? Provide them with props to turn your dramatic-play center into a construction zone! In advance, collect a few children's belts to transform into tool belts. To make a tool belt, cut a set of plastic six-pack rings in half lengthwise. Weave a belt in and out of one half (three rings); then hot-glue or staple the rings securely to the belt. Plastic toy tools can be slipped into the open spaces between the belt and the rings. Place the tool belts and other construction accessories—such as toy tools and dress-up hard hats—in your dramatic-play center.

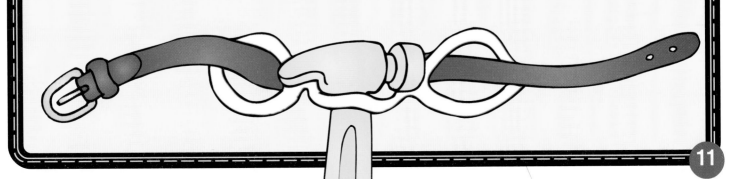

Dinosaurs

"Me-a-saurus"

Display pictures of dinosaurs in your block center. Point out various features to describe each dinosaur, such as the long tail, small head, and short front legs of an Apatosaurus. Then challenge your little ones to build their own dinosaurs using DUPLO® or LEGO® building blocks. When a dinosaur is complete, take an instant photo of it to display in the block center. Name each dinosaur after its designer; then write the name in the space below the photograph.

Charles-a-saurus

Dinosaurs Were Babies, Too!

Invite your little paleontologists to your sand table for a little dinosaur discovery. Purchase small plastic dinosaurs from a toy store. Or cut dinosaurs from thin craft sponge or craft foam. Place each dinosaur in a plastic egg; then bury the eggs in the sand table. Add some shovels to the table. Then invite youngsters to the center for a dinosaur dig. They're sure to dig the "egg-citing" discovery that awaits them!

Reptile Roll

Strengthen your little reptiles' counting skills with the roll of a die. To prepare, cut six notecards in half. Program each card with a dinosaur sticker or stamp; then place the cards in a basket. Put the basket in the math center along with a set of dice. Invite youngsters to roll the dice and count out the corresponding number of dinosaur cards. If desired, have younger children use only one die. Or add a third die and additional dinosaur cards to challenge more advanced students. Youngsters are sure to think this counting activity is "dino-mite"!

Fossil Finds

These dinosaur fossils are sure to leave a lasting impression. Place rolling pins and an assortment of small plastic or rubber dinosaurs in your play-dough center. Encourage your little paleontologists to roll out play-dough patties. Have them press the dinosaurs firmly into the patties, then remove them to discover the resulting imprints. After making several dinosaur impressions, encourage each fossil finder to match each of his dinosaurs to its fossil print. It's a find of a lifetime!

Prehistoric Estimation

Add some prehistoric splash to your water-table fun with this estimation activity. To prepare, cut islands of various sizes from colored Styrofoam® meat trays. Use a pencil to poke several holes in a few of the islands. Then put the islands, along with a quantity of small plastic dinosaurs, into your water table. Encourage each child to guess how many dinosaurs it will take to sink one of the islands. Then have her add one lovable lizard at a time to the island until it goes under water. Splash!

Fairy Tales

Royal Role-Play

Crown each child king or queen for some royal role-playing in the block center. To prepare, cover several tagboard crowns with aluminum foil; then staple the queen and king cards from a deck of playing cards to the crowns. Put the crowns and a few robes in your block center, along with some paper-towel-tube scepters. Invite youngsters in the center to dress as royalty; then have them construct a castle from blocks to house the royal family. Encourage the small groups of children to act out a regal fairy tale with the aid of their props. If desired, take photos to create a display showing off your youngsters' majestic imaginations.

Fairy-Tale Detectives

Stimulate youngsters' thinking skills with the push of a button—the button on your tape recorder, that is! To prepare for this listening-center activity, gather three fairy-tale books familiar to your children. Select several lines from the text of each tale that provide clues to the story. (Avoid choosing lines that include the title.) Make a tape recording of the chosen lines, using a bell to signal the end of the clues for each fairy tale. Place the tape and the three books in the listening center. Invite your little ones to listen carefully to the recording to identify the book corresponding to each set of clues. Then challenge youngsters to put the books in the order in which they heard the clues on the tape. (For younger students, you may want to include very specific directions on the tape, such as, "Those are all the clues for this story. Can you find this book?")

Going On A Bean Hunt

Youngsters will dig this sand-and-bean activity. To prepare, pour a bag of large dried beans (such as lima beans) into your sand table; then cover the beans with sand. Provide sifters, shovels, rakes, and a few miniature clay pots. After sharing *Jack And The Beanstalk* with your youngsters, explain that some of the beans landed right in your sand table when Jack's mother threw them out the window! Then have students in this center use the various tools to hunt for the beans and collect them in the pots. Invite each child to count the beans he finds.

I found 16 beans!

Trip-Trap Over The Bridge

Invite youngsters to role-play this troll play from *The Three Billy Goats Gruff.* In the block area, provide three goats from a toy farm set and one toy troll. Have small groups of children construct the troll's bridge from blocks. (If desired, invite your youngsters to build the bridge over a large tray of water.) When the bridge is complete, prompt the children to trip-trap their goats over the bridge in their own versions of this delightful tale.

A Tale Of Numbers

Here's a math activity that your youngsters are sure to think is number one! Prepare a tape recording of simple math problems based on various fairy tales. Begin the recording with the rhyme below; then follow the rhyme with a clue, such as, "The big bad wolf blew down this many houses." After a brief pause, repeat the rhyme followed by a different clue. Place the tape, a set of numeral cards labeled from 1–10, and a collection of corresponding fairy tales in your math center.

Invite student pairs to listen to each rhyme and clue on the tape. Have the children stop the tape after each clue to find the appropriate numeral card. If necessary, encourage youngsters to review the fairy-tale books to help them arrive at the correct answer.

I'm thinking of a number.
What number can it be?
It's in a special fairy tale.
Show that number to me.

Fall Harvest

Guess The Gourd

Use gourds to strengthen discrimination skills with this small-group activity that can become a center activity. To prepare, gather four gourds in a variety of sizes, shapes, textures, and weights. Invite children to explore each gourd using their senses. Encourage them to discuss how the gourds are alike and different. Then set the four gourds in front of one child. Give him a chance to observe the gourds; then blindfold him. Select one gourd for him to explore with his sense of touch. Then return the gourd to its original place. Remove the blindfold and have the child guess gourd which he was holding. Continue to blindfold other children at the center until all have had a chance to play Guess the Gourd. Once youngsters know how to play this guessing game, invite partners to play it in your discovery center.

"Weigh" To Go!

Here's a "weigh-cool" way to celebrate the fall harvest in your science center. Set up a balance scale next to an assortment of harvest foods, such as apples, small pumpkins, and gourds. Demonstrate how to use the scale if youngsters are unfamiliar with it. Then invite children to visit the center and explore the weights of the various harvest items. As you check in at the center, ask some questions to stimulate comparisons: Which item is heaviest? Which is lightest? Can students make any of the foods balance on the scale? Pound for pound, this center activity carries a lot of weight!

Impressions Of Fall

Add fall harvest foods to your play-dough center, and it's sure to make a lasting impression! Gather one or more of the following items: a walnut, an apple, an ear of Indian corn, and a miniature pumpkin. If you choose an apple, cut it in half to reveal the star in the center. Place the food items in a basket at your play-dough center. Provide a few rolling pins. Invite little ones to roll out some play dough, then press or roll each fall food into the dough to make an impression.

Pumpkin Portrait

Give youngsters an opportunity to strengthen fine-motor skills with this pumpkin-painting idea. To begin, spice up a cup of orange paint by adding a teaspoon of pumpkin pie spice to it. Then provide brown paint for the pumpkin stem, as well as some fat paintbrushes. Set an orange pumpkin on a chair by the easel. Then encourage each child to create a fine pumpkin portrait. If desired, display both a large and a small pumpkin; then challenge youngsters to capture the different-sized pumpkins on paper.

Bobbing Berries

Invite youngsters to your water table to try this unique harvesting technique. Explain to youngsters that growers harvest cranberries by flooding their fields and knocking the berries from the vines. The flood waters force the berries to float to the surface of the water so that the workers can collect them. Pour several bags of cranberries into the water table (the berries will float to the top). Provide strainers and a few harvesting scoops created from milk jugs; then have youngsters harvest the floating berries by scooping and depositing them into a strainer to drain. Be prepared for a "berry" good harvest!

Family

Mommy's Purse

Stuff a center with some of the treasures usually found stuffed in Mommy's purse! Gather a large purse, a wallet, keys, a pair of sunglasses, a comb, a notepad, a pen, and other items typically found in a pocketbook. Draw or trace each item on a tagboard card. Tape the cards to a table; then place each item in a separate sock and knot the end of the sock. Put the socks in the purse.

When a child visits this center, she removes a sock from the purse, feels its contents, and then places the sock on the card she believes matches its contents. After she empties the purse, she may empty the socks to check her guesses. Then she repacks each sock and repacks the purse so another curious youngster can discover the treasures in Mommy's purse.

Home Away From Home

Invite your little ones to create a dream home away from home in your block center. Encourage youngsters to construct a house of blocks. Provide toy people and doll furniture, and invite your little interior decorators to attach fabric-square curtains and carpet to the house to give it that homey feel. And don't forget to provide a toy cat or dog for the family pet. You might even suggest that youngsters build a doghouse for the dog. Everyone is sure to feel right at home in this center!

Kisses For Kin

This sandbox activity will encourage youngsters to pucker up for their loved ones. Put one Hershey's® Kisses® candy in each of ten or more lidded film canisters; then hide the canisters in your sand table. Hide some empty film canisters as well. Explain that the number of candies each child finds will be the number of *real* kisses she will give to her family members that evening. Then provide little ones with plastic sandwich bags in which to collect their candy. Invite pairs of children to take turns searching for the candy-filled canisters. After each child removes the candy, have her place the empty canister in a basket. Then refill the canisters with candy for the next pair that's ready to kiss and tell!

Chore Time

Youngsters will work their way into some household fun with this idea for your housekeeping center. To prepare, program each of several notecards with a picture of a common household tool or appliance to represent a different chore, such as a broom for sweeping, a feather duster for dusting, and a toy iron for ironing. Place the cards in the center, along with the appropriate items to perform each chore. Then invite small groups of children to dramatize being a family. Have each youngster select a chore card; then encourage the family members to work together to get the household chores done. It's family fun in the works!

My Gingerbread Family

Roll out some family fun at your play-dough center. To prepare, gather a collection of gingerbread-people cookie cutters of various sizes. Trace each cookie cutter on a supply of construction-paper; then cut out each outline, trimming away the hands, feet, and head so that the cutout resembles clothing. Place the cookie cutters, paper outfits, a garlic press, and colored sequins (or aquarium rocks) in your play-dough center.

Encourage each child to use the cookie cutters to create a play-dough person representing each member of her family. Invite her to dress each person in a paper outfit; then have her add sequin facial features. Encourage the child to create play-dough hair with the garlic press to make a special hairstyle for each family member. If desired, take a photograph of the play-dough family; then send the child home with the photo to show her real family.

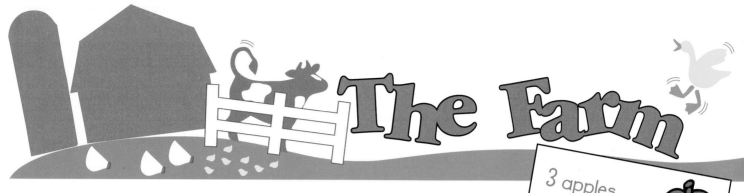

Barn-Raising Party

Raise some fun down on the farm with a barn-raising party. Tell your class that years ago barns were built by a team of farmers because it was a job too difficult for one to do alone. Then invite your little farmers to work in small teams to raise their own barns in the block center. Once each team has built its barn, invite the team to build fences for the plastic farm animals in the center. If desired, take an instant photo of each team enjoying its work and play around the barn. Then call in a demolition team to prepare the center for the next barn raising.

3 apples

2 broccoli

1 carrot

4 bananas

A Sing-Along Farmer Song

Your little ones will flock to the listening center to sing this special farmer's song—and be ready to come "baa-ck" for more later! In advance, make a tape recording of this song. Place the tape, along with the corresponding number of plastic animals named in the song, in your listening center. As youngsters visit the center, encourage them to round up the corresponding animals while quietly singing along to the tape.

(sung to the tune of "Old MacDonald Had A Farm")

[Teacher's name]'s class went to the farm,
E-I-E-I-O.
And at the farm we saw [one horse],
E-I-E-I-O.
With a [neigh-neigh] here, and a [neigh-neigh] there.
Here a [neigh], there a [neigh], everywhere a [neigh, neigh].
[Teacher's name]'s class went to the farm,
E-I-E-I-O.

Repeat the song, each time replacing the underlined number and animal with a different phrase: *two pigs, three sheep, four cows,* or *five chickens.* Also replace the animal sound with the sound corresponding to the named animal.

Farmer's Market

To market, to market, to buy a fat...fruit or vegetable! Transform your dramatic-play center into a farmer's market. Stock the center with baskets of plastic fruits and vegetables. (Or ask parents to send in real fruits and vegetables.) Then supply your marketplace with play money, a cash register, pencils and pads, grocery baskets, and paper bags. Next prepare individual shopping lists for your children to use at the market. On each list, program a designated number of items, such as 3 apples, 6 potatoes, and 4 pears. To facilitate independence in reading the list, illustrate each item; then put the lists in your marketplace. Finally, invite students to open their farmer's market for business. Encourage them to take turns shopping for the groceries on their lists, running the cash register, writing receipts, and bagging the produce. The market's open—come shop 'til you drop!

Center Scarecrow

A simple scarecrow will be the perfect centerpiece for your literacy center. Invite small groups of children, in turn, to help make a scarecrow. To create the head, draw a face on one side of an inverted paper grocery bag; then stuff the bag with newspaper. Glue raffia onto the head for hair. To make the scarecrow body, put a flannel shirt on a metal clothes hanger; then stuff the shirt with newspaper. Fit a pair of overalls over the shirt, attaching the straps to the shirt with safety pins. Then stuff the overalls with newspaper, too. Tuck the bottoms of the pant legs into a pair of sneakers. Attach the head to the body by inserting the hanger's hook into the bag, then tying it tightly in place with a length of raffia or string. Top off the head with a straw hat; then place the scarecrow on a chair in your literacy center.

As each youngster visits the center, invite her to read a story to this friendly scarecrow. Or have each youngster draw a picture of something that frightens her. Then encourage her to present the drawing to the scarecrow so that he can scare away the frightening thing.

All Sorts Of Farm Animals

Count on your little farmers to have all sorts of fun with this activity. Sup- ply your sand table with a large assortment of plastic farm animals. (Provide six or more of each type of animal.) Use plastic fence pieces from a toy farm set to make several fenced areas in the sand. Or use plastic berry baskets with the bottoms cut off. Place a Styrofoam® meat tray with a die near the sand table. Then instruct each youngster to roll the die onto the meat tray. Have him count out a number of identical animals corresponding to the number on the die. Then ask him to place the animals in a fenced area. Encourage your little ones to continue rolling, sorting, and counting until all the little piggies—and their pals—are in their pens!

21

The Five Senses

Construction "Sight"

Building observation skills is a snap with this block center idea. In advance, construct three simple structures using an assortment of blocks. Take an instant photo of each structure. Then take each structure apart and put each set of blocks in a separate box. Tape each photo to the box with the corresponding blocks. Have a child in this center select one of the boxes. After he studies the picture, ask him to reproduce the structure in the photo. Then invite him to exchange boxes with a fellow architect until he has had the opportunity to build each of the three structures. This is a true skill-building activity!

Tantalizing Taste Tests

Put your little ones' taste buds to the test at your discovery center. To prepare, list your students' names along the left side of a sheet of chart paper. Then create four columns to the right of the list. At the top of each column, draw a cookie, a pickle, a pretzel, or a square of unsweetened chocolate; then hang the chart in your discovery center. Provide samples of each of the foods on separate plates. Then invite each student to the center to taste each food. After he samples the food, have him mark his taste preferences on the chart by drawing a happy or sad face in the corresponding columns next to his name. Later, as a class, count the number of smiles and frowns to discover which foods passed—or failed—the taste test; then discuss the terms *sweet, sour, salty,* and *bitter.*

name	cookie	pickle	pretzel	chocolate
Georgia	:)	:(	:(	:(
Luke	:)	:(	:)	:(
Anthony	:)	:(	:)	:(
Caroline	:)	:(	:(	:)
Danielle	:)	:)	:(	:(
Charles	:)	:(	:(	:(
Frankie	:)	:)	:)	:(
Christine	:)	:(	:(	:(
Jamie	:)	:)	:)	:)

Polar Bear Club

Invite youngsters to your water table to discover animals belonging to the Polar Bear Club—those that live and play in the waters of the Arctic. To begin, add a bucket of ice cubes to your water table. Then add an assortment of plastic or rubber Arctic animals, such as polar bears, seals, and walruses. Invite your little explorers to play with the animals in the water. Encourage them to talk about the water's temperature and how life might be for the animals that live in and near such cold waters. For an added touch, teach youngsters this chant. Invite them to replace the underlined words with a different Arctic animal name each time they repeat the chant. Welcome to the Polar Br-r-r Club!

[Polar bear, polar bear], will you swim today?
The water's nice and cold. Hurray! Hurray!

Writing Makes "Scents"

Invite your little ones to use their sense of smell in the writing center, of all places! In advance, douse a few cotton balls with a distinctive scent, such as lemon or peppermint extract. Prepare several sets of cotton balls—each with a different scent—and allow all of them to dry. For each scent, label the front of a separate envelope with the scent's name and a picture clue. Then place each set of scented cotton balls in its corresponding envelope.

As each child visits this center, she chooses one envelope at a time. She sniffs the scent, then looks at the label and picture clue. She then draws a picture of what she smelled and, if capable, copies the name of the item onto her own paper.

What Made That Sound?

Help fine-tune your little ones' sense of hearing as they play this category game at the listening center. To prepare, make a tape of different animal and people sounds with ample pauses programmed between each sound. (You might record animal sounds such as a duck quacking, a dog barking, and a pig snorting, and your recorded people sounds might include laughing, crying, and sneezing.) Then divide a sheet of paper into two columns. Draw an animal at the top of one column and a person at the top of the other. Duplicate a copy for each child; then place the copies in the listening center along with the tape. As each youngster listens to the tape, encourage her to mark the appropriate column for each sound she hears—animal or person. Then have her compare her results with another child's. Shhh. Listen. What made that sound?

Friends

Painting Partners

Pair friends together as painting partners to double the fun of an ordinary fingerpainting activity. At the easel or art center, give each set of partners one large sheet of fingerpaint paper and a variety of fingerpaint colors. Encourage each pair to create one colorful work of art together. After the paintings dry, have each pair cut its painting in half so that each partner can take home a reminder of the fun shared between friends.

Paper-Doll Pals

Help youngsters identify their chain of friends with this fine-motor activity. For each child, fold a 9" x 18" piece of construction paper into thirds, so that it measures 9" x 6" folded. Trace a tagboard cutout of the paper-doll pattern (page 58) onto each folded paper as shown. Invite older students to cut around the outline, being careful not to cut through the arm folds. For younger students, cut out the patterns, creating a string of three paper dolls for each child. Invite each child to color each of her paper dolls to resemble a different classmate. Help her label each doll with the corresponding classmate's name. Send each child home with her paper-doll pals to introduce to her Mom and Dad.

Friendly Letters

The friendly notes written at this stationery factory are bound to manufacture some smiles. To prepare, take a close-up snapshot of each child's face. Photocopy the pictures; then cut them apart. Place the photocopied faces in the writing center; then add envelopes, stamps, stickers, and other decorating items to the center. Invite each child to create a sheet of customized stationery by decorating the outside edges of a sheet of paper with the provided supplies. Then encourage him to write (or dictate or draw) a note to a classmate on the stationery. Have him fold his note, insert it into an envelope, and then seal the envelope. Instruct the child to address the note by gluing the recipient's photocopied photo onto the front of the envelope. Then invite him to deliver the letter to his friend. After all your youngsters visit this center, each child will have written and received a friendly line. What a letter-perfect way to encourage writing—and smiles!

Listening To A "Lotto" Friends

Strengthen listening skills year-round with this friendly lotto game. Or use the game to help youngsters learn classmates' names at the beginning of the year. To begin, tape-record one child at a time saying, "Hi, preschool (or kindergarten) friends! Can you guess which friend I am?" Pause several seconds and then have the child record his name. To create a gameboard, glue individual student photographs onto a small poster board; then laminate the board. Place the gameboard and some bingo chips (or beans) in the listening center. To play, a child listens to each classmate's introduction on the tape. Then he puts a bingo chip on the photo of the child he believes to be the speaker. Can he guess the mystery classmate before that child reveals his name on the tape? In this game, a "lotto" friends turns into a "lotto" fun!

The Foundation Of Friendship

Use your block area to build a foundation for friendship through cooperation. Make a circle in the block center with yarn or a plastic hoop. Assign a small number of children to cooperatively build a block structure inside the circle. Be sure to praise the cooperation of the builders as they work together. When the structure is complete, ask the architects to describe their structure to their classmates. Then take a photo of the builders with their creation. Label the photo with the names of the featured children. After you have captured every team of builders on film, display all the photos on a bulletin board titled "Building Friendships With Cooperation."

Garden

Bees And Blooms

Invite youngsters to explore the "un-bee-lievable" relationship between the flower and the bee with this puppet rhyme. To begin, make a puppet stage by cutting out a window from the bottom of a large box (such as a copy-paper box); then paint the box green. After the paint dries, turn the box on its long side. Have students paint flowers on the box so that it resembles a flower garden. Next duplicate the bee and flower patterns (page 59) on tagboard. Color and cut out each pattern; then glue wiggle eyes to each cut-out. Tape each cutout to a craft-stick handle. Finally, tape-record this rhyme. Then place the stage, puppets, tape recorder, and tape in a center. Teach youngsters to use the puppets to perform the actions to the rhyme. Buzz!

Here's a pretty flower.   *Hold up flower.*
Here's a busy bee.   *Hold up bee.*
Each one needs the other,
You soon will surely see.

The flower needs the pollen   *Bee buzzes around the flower.*
The bee brings on her feet.
The bee needs the nectar
From flowers, oh so sweet.   *Bee lands on the flower.*

So when you see a buzzing bee,   *Hold up bee.*
Try not to make it "Shoo!"   *Make "shoo" motion.*
For it's honey from sweet nectar,
She's making just for you!   *Point to audience.*

Seeds To Sow

Your little sprouts will enjoy watching as seeds grow into plants in your own mini garden. In advance, buy a variety of seeds, such as tomatoes, lettuce, radishes, and lima beans. Purchase a few aluminum foil muffin tins. Put the seeds and pans in your science center, along with potting soil, index cards (cut in half), craft sticks, and a spray bottle of water. Invite each child to plant a seed of his choice. Have him label a card with his name, then draw a picture of what his plant will look like when it's grown. Help him glue the card to a craft stick, then insert the stick into the muffin cup containing his seed. As a class, care for the mini garden until the seedlings are ready to be transplanted outdoors. Then cut the foil cups apart. Send each plant home with its owner to plant in his personal garden.

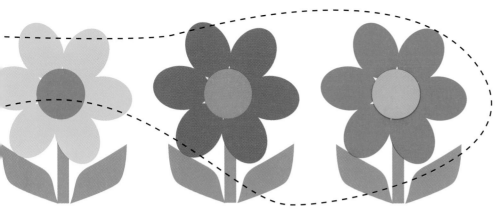

Play-Dough Posies (And Roses And Tulips And Daisies...)

Creativity will stem from this play-dough activity. In advance, gather several pastel colors of play dough. Provide flower-shaped cookie cutters and green pipe cleaners. Then invite children to cut out or create their own play-dough flowers. Show them how to roll small balls of dough and flatten them to create flower centers and petals. Encourage them to complete their flowers with pipe-cleaner stems and leaves.

Sand Table Garden

Have your little gardeners put their green thumbs to the test in your sand table. To prepare, collect children's plastic garden tools, garden gloves, straw hats, a watering can, a water-filled spray bottle, and several plastic flowers. Place the items near your sand table. As children visit the center, encourage them to dress in the hats and gloves for a day of gardening. Invite them to wet the "soil" with the spray bottle, then "plant" the flowers in the sand. Then have them pretend to water the flowers with the watering can. My, what a unique garden!

Glorious Garden

Your budding artists will plant themselves in the art center to make this floral mural. To prepare, cut a length of white bulletin-board paper to use as the background. Gather a soft nylon shower "scrunchie," a foam dish mop, several lengths of corrugated bulletin-board border, and bowls of paint. Roll up each bulletin-board border tightly; then secure each roll with a rubber band. Cover an area of the floor with newspaper. Then place the paper and other materials on the newspaper. Encourage youngsters to dip the scrunchie, the dish mop, and the flat ends of the rolled border in paint, then press them onto the paper to create flowers. After the paint dries, have youngsters draw stems and leaves for their flowers. Display your mural in the hall; then watch the compliments bloom!

27

Health & Safety

Signs Of Safety

Give your little ones a reason to STOP and notice traffic signs by making your own for the block center. To begin, draw an assortment of road signs—such as *Stop, Yield, Speed Limit,* and *Railroad Crossing*—on appropriate tagboard shapes. (Or, for an even more realistic look, cut the signs from a driver's handbook; then mount the cutouts on tagboard.) Glue each sign to one end of a craft stick. Use plaster of paris to anchor the other end of each craft stick inside a plastic top from a laundry detergent bottle. After the plaster dries, place the signs in your block center. They're sure to be real traffic stoppers!

Wash Those Hands!

Set up your discovery center to help youngsters discover the importance of washing their hands. Provide brown tempera paint, several brushes, a supply of paper towels, and a supply of white copy paper. Invite a child who visits the center to first label a sheet of paper with his name. Then have him paint the palm of one hand with the brown paint. Have him wipe his hand off with a paper towel, then make a handprint on one side of his paper. Then have him go to the sink, wash his hands with soap and water, and dry them. Have him return to the center and make another handprint next to the first one. If the paint were dirt, which method was more effective in removing it—wiping his hands or washing them? If desired, print the message "Wash Those Hands!" on each child's paper and send it home to spark a discussion.

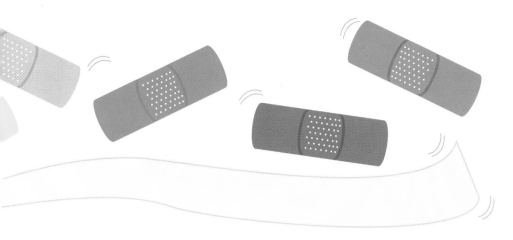

What's Up, Doc?

Doctor up your drama center by setting up a medical clinic. To begin, gather several toy doctor kits. Or ask the school nurse or parents in the medical profession to donate items such as lab coats (or oversized, white dress shirts), plastic syringes, empty pill bottles, stethoscopes, gauze, bandages, and ice packs. Place the supplies in your dramatic-play center. Set up a few chairs to serve as the waiting room area and a cot or nap mat to use as the examination table for patients. Ready? The doctor is in!

Red Light, Green Light

Students will *stop* what they're doing to *go* to this safety-awareness center! In advance, make a tagboard copy of the safety cards on page 60; then color and cut apart the cards. If desired, laminate them for durability. Open a manila file folder and draw a red circle on one side of the fold and a green circle on the other side to represent traffic lights. Store the picture cards inside the folder. Invite each youngster who visits this center to open the folder and sort the cards. Have him place the cards that show safe actions on the green traffic light and the cards that show unsafe actions on the red traffic light. After this activity, youngsters will be "en-light-ened" about safety!

Erasing Cavities

Help little ones brush up on dental hygiene with this center activity that's guaranteed to make them smile. To begin, affix pieces of white plastic tape to your chalkboard to create a big, toothy grin. Cut out a tagboard toothbrush about the size of a chalkboard eraser; then tape the cutout to the back of a chalkboard eraser. Invite visitors to the center to use colored chalk to draw particles of food on and between the white-tape teeth. Then have them use the toothbrush-eraser to brush off the traces of cavity-forming foods. Let's see those pearly whites now!

Leaves

Leaves That Measure Up

Set up this handy center to reinforce the concept of size. Collect a basketful of fresh fall leaves of varied sizes. Then trace your hand twice at the top of a large sheet of paper. Glue a leaf onto each hand outline—one leaf that is smaller than the hand, and one that is larger than the hand. Sort a few more leaves by this criteria and glue each one to the paper on the corresponding side. Place the paper in your math center, along with the basket of leaves, glue, crayons, and large sheets of paper.

To use the center, a student traces his hand twice on paper. He measures some leaves against his own hand to determine whether the leaves are larger or smaller than his hand; then he glues the leaves in place to create a leaf project similar to the display.

Float 'n' Sort

An "as-sort-ment" of fall fun awaits your youngsters with this water table activity. To prepare, cut a variety of leaf shapes and sizes from autumn colors of craft foam. Place the foam leaves in the water table along with a few Styrofoam® meat trays. Encourage children to sort the floating leaves by color, shape, or size onto the meat trays. Then have them dump the leaves back into the water for more sorting fun.

Colors Of Autumn

Give your youngsters a preview of the colors of autumn with this paint-and-press project. Collect large, supple, green leaves during the last days of summer. Then discuss what will soon happen to green leaves as fall weather approaches. Stock the art center with white construction paper, fat paintbrushes, and autumn colors of paint, such as brown, orange, and yellow. Instruct each student to paint the vein side of a leaf, then press the painted leaf onto a sheet of white paper. Have her carefully lift the leaf to reveal a colorful leaf print. Encourage her to repeat the process using a variety of colors and overlapping the prints. Your little ones will leave this center with a colorful image of what lies ahead.

Tasty Leaves

Your little ones won't "be-leaf" their ears when you invite them to eat leaves at this teacher-directed center. Purchase a bag of mixed salad greens; then pour the greens into a large clear bowl. Explain to a small group of youngsters that—although they should never pluck a leaf from a houseplant or nibble on a tree leaf in the yard—the leaves of many plants *are* edible. Pass the bowl around for little ones to observe the edible leaves. Give each child a leaf to touch and hold. As the children examine the leaves, record their comments about the looks, smell, and feel of their leaves on a large leaf cutout. Then give each child a few salad greens on a paper plate. (If desired, provide salad dressing for dipping.) As little ones gobble their greens, add their comments about the taste of the leaves to your leaf cutout. Yummy!

Leaves are green. **Luke**
They smell fresh. **Katie**
They're soft. **Danielle**
Some of them are crunchy.
Alex

Leaf Match

Are your youngsters game for a little leaf viewing? To prepare this leaf-matching game, duplicate the desired number of leaf gameboards (page 61) on construction paper. To make different versions of the gameboard, cut the boards so that each one has only nine squares, as shown. Then enlarge one uncut copy of the gameboard and cut apart the 16 squares to serve as game cards. Laminate the gameboards and cards; then place them in a center along with a supply of plastic bingo chips.

At this center, each child in a small group takes a gameboard. One child takes the leaf cards and holds up one card at a time. After carefully viewing the card on display, each player marks the matching leaf on his gameboard with a bingo chip. Continue the game until one player covers all the leaves on her gameboard (or until everyone has covered all her leaves).

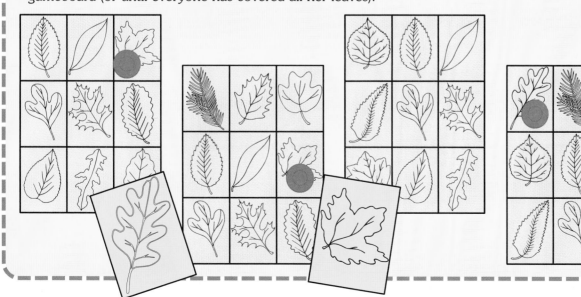

New Year

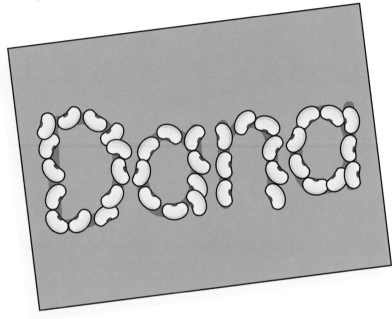

Good-Luck Peas

Some people believe that if a person eats black-eyed peas on New Year's Day, he will have good luck all year long. Explain this tradition to youngsters; then surprise them with a sensory tub full of dried black-eyed peas. Place the tub in a center along with some measuring cups, funnels, and scoops to encourage free exploration. After students have had time to explore, give each child a cotton swab, glue, and a piece of heavy cardboard labeled with his name. Encourage him to trace his name with a cotton swab dipped in glue. Then have him place peas along the glue lines to spell out his name. Now, that's luck that's bound to stick!

Top Off The New Year

Crown each of your youngsters King (or Queen) of the New Year. Supply your art center with a sentence strip for each child, pencils with erasers, pie tins filled with paint, sponge numerals to represent the New Year, and lengths of curling ribbon. To make a crown, each youngster sponge-paints the New Year's numerals onto a sentence strip. Then he dips the eraser end of a pencil into paint and prints confetti circles of various colors onto the strip. As a finishing touch, he glues lengths of curled ribbon to his crown. After the crown dries, staple the ends together to fit the child's head. In ceremonial fashion, present each child with his personalized crown; then wish him a New Year fit for a king!

Coin Cakes

Send some luck your little ones' way in your play-dough center. Explain to the children that some New Year's celebrations include a cake baked with a coin inside it. The person who gets the piece of cake with the coin will be lucky all year. At the play-dough table, provide regular and mini cupcake pans, as well as a small basket of shiny new pennies. Then invite youngsters to prepare play-dough cupcakes, some with and some without coins hidden inside. When the next group visits the center, challenge them to guess which cupcakes contain the coins. Have the children crumble the cupcakes to find and remove the coins. Then have that group "cook up" another dozen or more lucky coin cakes.

A Celebration Collage

Here's a great way to recycle the old to celebrate the new. In advance, send a note to parents requesting that they save leftover party decorations from their New Year's celebrations to send to class. If desired, provide a wish list of items, such as confetti, streamers, paper plates, cups, party hats, and blowers. Put the party supplies in the art center with sheets of brightly colored construction paper and glue. Then invite youngsters to make a New Year's collage using the recycled party supplies. Happy New Year!

Build A New Year

Invite your little architects to design a bit of New Year's excitement with this block center idea. Challenge them to construct the numerals representing the New Year using wooden blocks, LEGO® blocks, Flexiblocks, or other building materials. For the child who might have difficulty forming the numerals, provide a poster board labeled with large numerals representing the year. Have youngsters place the poster board on the floor, then position their blocks atop the numerals. Watch how the New Year takes shape!

Nursery Rhymes

Mime-And-Rhyme Time

Set the stage for your little actors to give award-winning performances with this idea. Collect items to create nursery-rhyme prop boxes. For example, you might put a bowl, a spoon, and a plastic spider in a box labeled "Little Miss Muffet." Or mittens, cat-ear headbands, and a pie pan might be in a box for "Three Little Kittens." Place the boxes in a center; then use colored tape to mark off an area for a stage. Place a few chairs in front of the stage for the audience. Then invite small groups of youngsters to use the props to silently act out the nursery rhymes, while students in the audience try to identify the rhyme. After the correct rhyme is named, have the actors repeat their performance as the audience recites the rhyme. As you introduce each new rhyme, place a corresponding prop box in the center for more miming and rhyming fun.

"Hickory, dickory, dock!"

Rhymes In A Box

Use an accessory box to build nursery-rhyme activity in your block area. Fill the box with items to represent nursery rhymes of your choice. For example, put in a plastic sheep and play people to represent "Mary Had A Little Lamb," and a small stuffed mouse and a toy clock for "Hickory Dickory Dock." Then have youngsters build block structures to go along with the rhymes, such as Mary's schoolhouse or a tall grandfather clock. Invite children to use the props and the block structures to enhance their nursery-rhyme play.

Reciting Rhymes

Here's a way to get youngsters excited about listening to nursery rhymes. Tape-record individual children, each reciting or singing a favorite nursery rhyme. Place the tape at your listening center, along with a book of nursery rhymes. Invite youngsters to listen to each rhyme on the tape, then to find that rhyme in the nursery-rhyme book. For an additional challenge, ask youngsters to try to name the classmate who recites each rhyme.

My Own Nursery-Rhyme Book

Have youngsters create their own collection of traditional nursery rhymes with this activity. On separate sheets of paper, write or type the words to each rhyme learned during your nursery-rhyme unit. Duplicate a class supply of each rhyme. Then, after you introduce each rhyme to your class, place copies of that rhyme in the art center. Invite each child to the center to illustrate the rhyme. Collect the illustrations and save them in a file. At the end of your unit, collate and bind each child's drawings between tagboard covers. Have each youngster decorate his cover with nursery-rhyme stickers; then invite him to take his book home to enjoy some readin' and rhymin' with relatives.

Jack be nimble.
Jack be quick.
Jack jump over the candlestick.

Humpty Dumpty sat on a wall.

Humpty Dumpty had a great fall.

All the king's horses and all the king's men.

Couldn't put Humpty together again.

Line-By-Line Rhymes

Order up some rhyming fun with this prereading activity. Write the words to "Humpty Dumpty" or another nursery rhyme on chart paper. (If desired, use rebus pictures for younger children.) Write each line from the rhyme on a separate sentence strip. Display the complete rhyme in a center; then place the sentence strips near the rhyme. Ask youngsters to put the strips in order, using the chart as a guide. After the children have had success sequencing the sentence strips, cut the strips into short phrases or single words. Then invite all your king's men (and women) to put the rhyme together again!

Nutrition

Fruit And Veggie Kabobs

Thread together some fine-motor fun with these fruit and veggie kabobs. To prepare, place a class quantity of each of these foods on separate plates: halved seedless grapes, strawberry halves, melon chunks, celery slices, cucumber slices, and red pepper strips. Set out paper plates and wooden skewers. Provide supervision at this center, where a child may thread her fruits and vegetables onto her skewer to make a tasty—and nutritious—treat. If desired, challenge older students to thread the fruits and vegetables in an alternating pattern. It's a center...it's a snack...it's a great idea!

Prints With A Purpose

Here's an art center activity that puts the food groups in print. To prepare, gather the following printing items to represent each of the six food groups: an apple (cut in half), a broccoli stalk (cut in half), a sponge cut to resemble a slice of Swiss cheese, a sponge cut to resemble a bread slice, a sponge cut into the shape of a fish, and a sponge cut into the shape of a candy cane. Place each food or sponge on a separate paper plate; then put them on the art table with several pie tins of paint and a class supply of 12" x 18" white construction paper. Instruct each youngster at this center to dip each printing item into the paint and then press it onto her construction paper. When the paint is dry, send these printing projects home as a reminder of the six food groups.

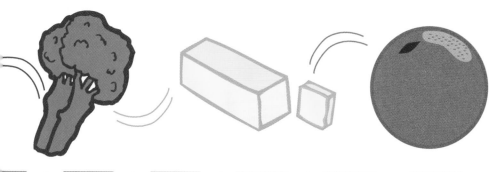

Mystery Foods

An understanding of nutrition is bound to rub off on your students with these food rubbings. To prepare, gather the following items: uncooked elbow macaroni, a dried apple ring, raw carrot rounds, a wrapped slice of Swiss cheese, unshelled sunflower seeds, an unwrapped Hershey's® candy bar, six index cards, six envelopes, and a bottle of rubber cement. Use the rubber cement to attach each food to a separate index card. When the rubber cement is dry, insert each food card into a separate envelope. Seal the envelopes and place them on a table with unwrapped crayons and thin drawing paper.

When a child visits this center, he takes one of the mystery envelopes, places a piece of drawing paper on top of it, and then gently rubs the side of a crayon over the paper until an image of the food appears. Invite youngsters to do crayon rubbings of all six envelopes, and challenge them to guess the foods contained in each one. After all your children have visited the center, take the mystery out of nutrition by revealing the envelopes' contents and discussing the food group to which each food belongs.

Shopping List
- apple
- banana
- milk
- chicken
- bread

Selective Shoppers

Help your little shoppers select healthful foods with these nutritious grocery lists. In advance, choose a large selection of nutritious play foods from your kitchen area. Next, cut a number of 3" x 12" rectangles from white construction paper. Label the top of each strip "Shopping List." (Or use sheets from a purchased shopping list pad.) On each sheet, draw and label pictures of some of the healthful foods you've set aside. Make up several lists with a variety of items; then laminate them for durability. Place the play foods, the lists, some grocery bags, a toy shopping cart or basket, a cash register, a purse, a wallet, and play money in your dramatic-play center. Invite youngsters to pay a visit to this makeshift grocery store to purchase healthful foods from one of the shopping lists.

The "Weigh" To Nutrition

This math center activity will show students that good nutrition carries a lot of weight! In a center, set out a balance scale, a supply of counters, and a variety of healthful foods, such as an orange, a cucumber, a potato, a wrapped wedge of cheese, and a zippered bag of raisins. Encourage children in this center to weigh the foods with counters and to compare the weights of the various foods to one another. Youngsters will enjoy weighing the possibilities!

Ocean

Down By The Sea

Youngsters will be more than willing to dive into this alluring book-and-beach center. To prepare, fill the shelves of your reading center with books about the beach or ocean. Adorn the walls of the center with fishnets and sea-life posters. Add that seaside feeling with items such as a beach umbrella (you might sink the umbrella handle into a large, heavy clay pot of plaster of paris), a beach chair, some floats, and a beach bag containing an empty bottle of sunscreen, sun visors, sunglasses, flip-flops, goggles, and a beach towel. If desired, also add a small kiddie pool. Then place a tape recorder and a tape of beach sounds in the center. Then invite youngsters to soak up a few rays while engaging in some sizzlin'-hot summer reading at the beach.

Collecting Seashells

Your little ones will be as happy as clams with this counting activity. To prepare, make a tagboard tracer of the sand-pail pattern on page 62. (You don't need the fish pattern for this activity.) Use a black permanent marker to trace the pattern several times onto a Formica® tabletop, adding the handle detail. (Or make tagboard sand pails, laminate them, and tape them to a table in your math center.) Use the permanent marker to program each pail with a numeral from 1 to 10. Put a real sand pail full of seashells on the table. Then encourage your little shell seekers to count out the number of shells corresponding to the numeral on each sand pail. For variety, change the numerals on the pails each day. To erase the sand pails, simply wash the table with alcohol; then gently scrub away any remaining stains with Comet®. Only the learning will be permanent!

Sea Sights And Sounds

This imaginary seaside expedition is bound to reel youngsters into your discovery center. Gather ocean-related items, such as an assortment of shells, starfish, sharks' teeth, seagull feathers, sea horses, coral, and seaweed. If possible, add a crab or lobster shell to the collection. (You might request these from the seafood department of your grocery store.) Fill the top of a large, deep gift box with a layer of sand. Place the sea items in the sand along with a magnifying glass. Then invite youngsters to discover the treasures of the sea.

Oceans Of Bubbles

Are you fishing for a project to make your youngsters bubble over with enthusiasm? Then try this seaworthy project in your art area. In advance, use the fish pattern on page 62 to cut a few fish shapes from thin craft sponge. In your art center, set out cookie sheets, cups of bubble solution, straws, blue food coloring, half-sheets of white construction paper, the fish-shaped sponges, and shallow trays of tempera paint. Each child who visits the center first writes his name on a half-sheet of paper. He then places a cup of bubble solution atop a cookie sheet. He adds 10–12 drops of blue food coloring to his cup, then uses a straw to blow bubbles in his cup until they rise above the rim. He places his personalized piece of paper on top of the cup to capture the bubble prints, then sets his paper aside to dry. He may revisit the center later to make fish-shaped sponge prints on the bubbly water background.

Ships Ahoy!

Invite each of your little sailors to captain his very own boat at the water table. Put a box of LEGO® or DUPLO® blocks near the water table along with some DUPLO® people. Encourage the children to put the building blocks together to make their own floating vessels. Encourage them to man their ships with toy people posing as ship captains, fishermen, or passengers. Then challenge each youngster to brainstorm ways to sail his boat from one end of the water table to the other without touching the boat. A child might suggest that he blow his boat across the water or create waves to push his boat across. Invite him to try out some of his ideas. It's plain to "sea" that creativity will be afloat at this center!

Rain

Rain Gear

Gear up for wet weather by stocking your dramatic-play center with rainy-day attire. In advance, ask parents to send in rain gear, such as galoshes, ponchos, boots, rain hats, and slickers. (You may want to discourage parents from sending in umbrellas, since they can be a bit hazardous during free play.) Encourage parents to label articles of clothing with their children's names. Add the items to your dramatic-play center. Laminate puddles cut from blue construction paper; then tape them to the floor for "splashing." Ask youngsters to name the various articles of clothing as they parade around in their puddle-stompin' gear.

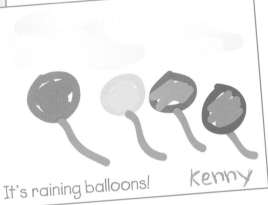

It's raining balloons! Kenny

Cloudy With A Chance Of "Brainstorms"

The forecast for this idea calls for a flood of imagination! To prepare, place a bag of colored cotton balls, glue, crayons, and white construction paper in your art center. Demonstrate for students how to stretch a cotton ball to create a cloud. Then have each child stretch and glue wispy clusters of cotton-ball clouds onto a sheet of white construction paper. After students create their clouds, encourage them to draw imaginative items falling from the clouds. Ask each youngster to describe his drawing to you; then record his descriptions on his paper. Be sure to batten down the hatches for the brainstorms headed your way!

Counting In The Rain

Give little fingers a workout counting raindrops. Supply a center with eyedroppers, clear plastic cups, and numerals cut from craft foam. Partially fill some of the cups with blue-tinted water. Demonstrate for students how to use an eyedropper to transfer water from a water-filled cup to an empty one. Allow students at this center to experiment and practice using their eyedroppers. Then have each child pour all his water back into one cup. Instruct him to select a numeral from the basket; then have him drop the corresponding number of raindrops into his empty cup. Encourage him to continue in this manner until he's enjoyed the last drop!

Rain Check

Take advantage of a rainy day by checking out some raindrops. When the forecast calls for rain, set up your discovery center with a cup, blue food coloring, an eyedropper, a spoon, toothpicks, and waxed paper. Invite small groups to observe single raindrops as they travel down a classroom windowpane and collide with other drops. Then send a child out to collect some rainwater in the cup. Mix blue food coloring into the rainwater to make it more visible. Then provide each child with a toothpick and a piece of waxed paper. Using the eyedropper, put a few drops of rainwater on each child's waxed paper. Encourage each child to explore the drops with his toothpick. Can he make the drops wiggle or break into smaller drops? Can he combine all the drops into one large raindrop? The forecast for this activity is clear—wet and wild!

From Drizzle To Downpour

Shower your students with some rainy-day vocabulary at your water table. To prepare, remove the lids from three whipped-topping containers; then punch holes in the bottom of each container. Make tiny holes in the first container, medium-sized holes in the second, and large holes in the last container. Place the containers in your water table. Introduce your youngsters to some words that describe rain, such as *sprinkle, drizzle, shower,* or *downpour.* Then encourage them to visit your water table for a demonstration. Invite children to fill the different containers with water, hold them above the water table, and then determine what kind of rain results from each one. Pitter-patter. Drip-drop. Splish-splash!

Self-Awareness

Name And Number, Please

Try this activity to reinforce name recognition, visual discrimination, letter recognition, or counting skills. To prepare, write the letters of each child's name on a sentence strip, leaving ample space between letters. Trim the excess off each sentence strip. Program index cards, each with a different numeral from 2 to 12. Put the name strips and numeral cards in a box; then place the box in a center.

Invite youngsters who visit this center to find their name strips and use them for all sorts of learning! Encourage each child to count the letters in her name (or someone else's) and then to find the corresponding numeral card. Invite youngsters to group names according to similar characteristics, such as those that begin or end with the same letter, or those that have the same number of letters. Names and numbers—neat!

Handprint Hello

Here's a handy way for youngsters to send some personalized greetings to the world. Cover the floor beneath a classroom window with newspaper. Pour colorful tempera paints (with a bit of dish detergent mixed in) into shallow trays; then place the trays on the newspaper. Have each child dip his hand into the paint and then create a handprint on a windowpane. Encourage youngsters to decorate the entire window with their colorful handprints. After the paint dries, ask each child to measure his hand against the prints on the window to find his own unique handprints. Can he find other handprints that are larger or smaller than his? Paint the title "Preschool Waves Hello" (backward, of course!) on the window to provide a warm greeting for all who walk by.

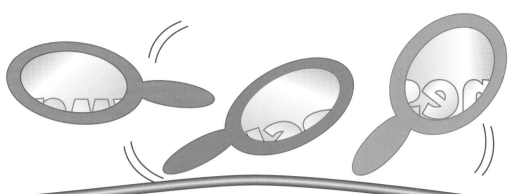

Color Me Beautiful!

Have youngsters show their true colors with this unique form of self-expression. Set up a center with tabletop mirrors or hand mirrors. Provide face paints or face-painting crayons. As each child visits the center, encourage her to paint her face and then to examine the colorful results in the mirror. Take a photograph of each child to display with the title "Color Me Beautiful!"

I Am Special

Help each child get started with this art-center activity. To prepare, gather a class supply of 12" x 18" white construction paper. Program the bottom of each sheet with "I am special because _____." Then ask each child to tell you what makes her a special person. Complete the sentence at the bottom of her page with her response; then ask the child to take her page to the art center and illustrate it. Collect and bind the finished pages into a class book. Share the book with the class to celebrate individual differences. Then invite each child, in turn, to take the class book home to share with parents.

Oh, How I've Grown!

Instill pride beyond measure with this fun math-center activity. To prepare, send home a note asking that parents jot down their child's length at birth and return this information to you. Then cut a four-foot length of bulletin-board paper for each child. Program each child's paper as shown, drawing a line corresponding to her height at birth on the left side. Leave ample room on the right side of the paper. Place all the papers, along with crayons and same-sized wooden unit blocks, in a center.

Invite pairs of children to visit this center. Have each child lie on the right side of her paper while her partner traces around her body. Then have her use the unit blocks to measure the line and determine her birth height in blocks. Have her measure her body outline to find her current height in blocks. Help her record the number of blocks used for each measurement. If desired, have each child color her body outline to resemble herself.

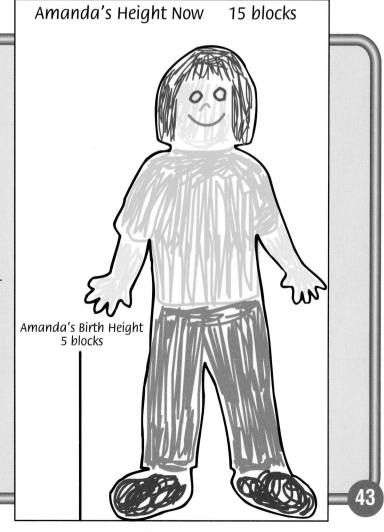

Amanda's Height Now   15 blocks

Amanda's Birth Height
5 blocks

SNOW

Snow Snips

Here's a cool and easy way for youngsters to make their own unique snowflakes at your art center. Stock the center with a large supply of coffee filters and several pairs of scissors. Show students how to fold a coffee filter three times to create a triangle. Then demonstrate how to snip away pieces from the sides of the triangle without cutting away an entire folded side. Unfold the coffee filter to reveal a unique snowflake. Students will create a flurry of snowflakes in no time at all!

To Eat Or Not To Eat?

Children love to snack on snow, but is it clean enough to eat? To find out, set up a snow investigation center after a fresh snowfall. Prepare a snow-melting jar by pushing a large coffee filter into the top of a wide-mouthed jar to create a cup inside the jar. Secure the filter to the rim of the jar with a rubber band. Then collect a few cups of snow. Encourage the children to look closely at the snow and describe what they see. Place a scoop of snow in the coffee filter; then allow the snow to melt. Have children explore other centers while the snow melts, reminding them to periodically check the snow as it changes from a solid to a liquid. After the snow has melted completely, remove the coffee filter from the jar. Have students inspect the filter for color and debris. After this experiment, your students will conclude that snow only *looks* good enough to eat.

Sensational Sensory Snow

Invite youngsters to have mounds of fun with some faux snow. Remove the chairs from a classroom table so students can stand around it, and then protect the floor beneath the table with a sheet or newspaper. Squirt several mounds of shaving cream on the table and invite youngsters at the center to enjoy the piles of faux snow. Encourage children to draw in the snow or write letters, numerals, or their names. If desired, provide snowman cookie cutters. Every once in a while, create a fresh snowfall by squirting more shaving cream onto the table. When it's time to clean up for the next snow crew, just plow the mess away with the wipe of a wet cloth. It's guaranteed to be "snow" much fun—without the cold!

Shimmering "Snowdough"

Add some seasonal sparkle to your play-dough area with this glistening glitter snow. In advance, use your favorite recipe to make a batch of play dough, without adding color to it. Then sprinkle a layer of iridescent glitter on your play-dough table. Ask youngsters to roll the fresh batch of dough in the glitter. Encourage them to observe how the glitter adheres to the play dough, making it sparkle. Then invite youngsters to use their "snowdough" to form some sparkly snow creations.

Snow Matters

Use these cool cubes to help your little ones experience the meltdown of a solid into a liquid. To prepare, make a thin mixture of white tempera paint and water. Pour the thin paint into ice-cube trays; then add a craft stick to each cup. (Make at least one cube per student.) Place the trays in the freezer overnight. The next day, remove the paint cubes from the trays.

Place a few cubes in your art center; then return the remaining cubes to the freezer until students are ready to use them. Invite each youngster at the center to paint on a sheet of blue or black paper with a paint cube. As you circulate, ask youngsters to describe the changes in the cubes as they paint. What a beautiful meltdown!

Space

Stick With The Stars

Before your intergalactic explorers take off for the moon, they'll need to practice the countdown to liftoff with this center activity. Program each of ten wide craft sticks with a different number of foil stars from one to ten. To prevent the stars from peeling off, paint the craft sticks with a light coat of clear fingernail polish. Then use a permanent marker to program each of ten additional craft sticks with a numeral from 1 to 10. Place both sets of craft sticks in a center. Invite each space traveler to match each star stick to its corresponding numeral stick. Then challenge youngsters to sequence the sticks in reverse order from ten to one. Ready? Ten, nine, eight…

Let's Visit The Planetarium!

Launch into space exploration with your own planetarium, made from a refrigerator box. If desired, enlist the help of your students to paint the exterior of the box black. After the paint dries, remove one end of the box. Have youngsters crawl inside and attach glow-in-the-dark stars to the interior of the box. Then invite them to use glow-in-the-dark crayons to create their own stars and planets on the inside and outside of the box. Cut a flap large enough to crawl through at the cutaway end of the box. Stand the box on its cutaway end, and have one space explorer at a time visit the planetarium to view the stars and planets. After each child's visit, have him use glow-in-the-dark crayons to draw his observations on black construction paper. Your youngsters will be starstruck in this center!

Star Light, Moon Bright

Invite your young stargazers to create their own starry-night pictures with this art-center activity. Supply the center with 12" x 18" sheets of black construction paper, small paper plates, and star stickers. Also add glue, paintbrushes, and a glitter-paint mixture of yellow paint and gold or iridescent glitter. When a child visits this center, she creates a moon by painting a paper plate with the glitter paint. When the paint dries, she glues her moon to a sheet of black construction paper; then she adds star stickers to the paper. Display the finished night-sky creations on your classroom ceiling to create a glorious galaxy.

Journey Into Outer Space

Watch your youngsters' enthusiasm rocket sky-high at this sensory table. To prepare, lay a sheet of bubble wrap under a layer of sand in your sand table. Then add Styrofoam® materials, such as packing pieces, balls of different sizes, and cups or bowls. Provide pipe cleaners and straws cut into different lengths. Then invite youngsters to use their imaginations—and the provided materials—to create everything from spaceships and planets to aliens and flying saucers.

Space: The Final "Fun-tier"

Dress up your dramatic-play center for imaginary explorations into space. To prepare, provide dress-up items to represent articles that an astronaut might wear, such as an oversized gray sweat suit, heavy work gloves, adult's rubber boots, a headset from your listening center, goggles, and a bike helmet. Then invite your little space travelers to suit up and take off on an imaginary space adventure!

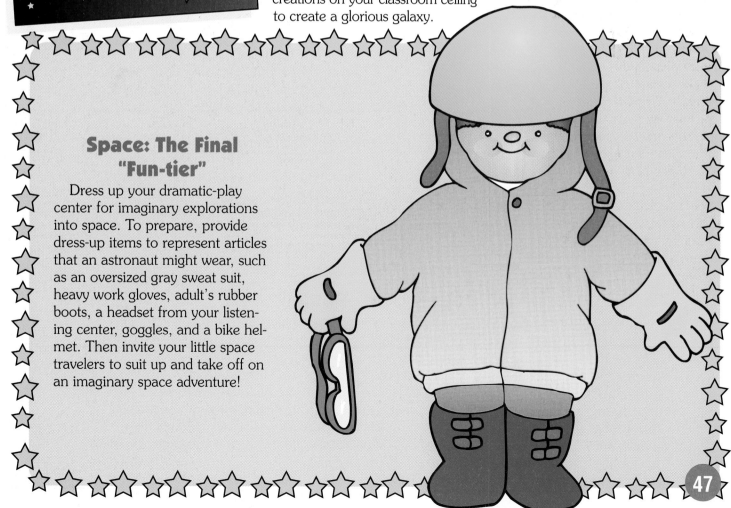

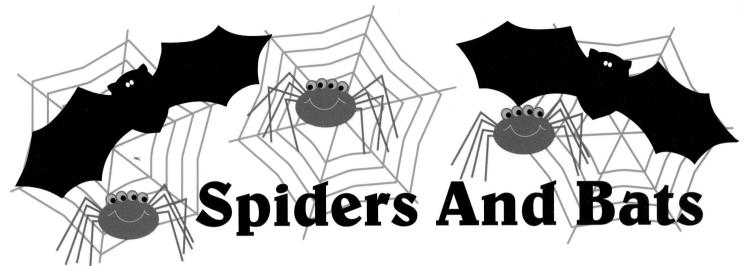

Spiders And Bats

I think this is a marble!

Bat Sense

If you look at a picture of a bat, you'll notice that its ears are large compared to the size of its body. Large ears help the bat hear better. Bats use their unique sense of hearing to help them navigate and find food. Invite your youngsters to test *their* sense of hearing with this sensory activity. Collect eight black film canisters; then sort the canisters into pairs. Fill each canister in a pair with an identical item, such as a cotton ball, a penny, a paper clip, or a marble. (Be certain the four pairs of canisters each have different contents.) Fasten the lids onto the canisters; then place them in your discovery center. Also add to the center an envelope containing a sample of the four different items in the canisters.

Invite children who visit this center to use their sense of hearing to do some sound matching. Have them shake the canisters and try to match the pairs by sound. To extend the activity, ask students to place each item from the envelope with the corresponding canister pair. Then have them remove the canister lids to confirm their guesses.

Blind As A...Spider?

Well, actually, most spiders aren't blind. But web-weaving spiders do have poor eyesight; yet they can weave beautiful and intricate webs! Have your little ones imitate spiders' web-weaving abilities with this fine-motor center. To prepare, purchase some six-inch black paper plates. Use a hole puncher to make holes around the perimeter of each plate. Thread a length of white yarn through one of the holes in each plate; then tie the end in place. Wrap tape around the loose ends of the yarn lengths (for ease in lacing). Place the prepared plates in your fine-motor center.

Encourage each youngster at this center to pick up a plate, close his eyes, and attempt to weave a web by "sewing" the yarn in and out of the holes in the plate. (If desired, provide blindfolds for youngsters to wear as they weave.) When he comes to the end of his yarn, have him open his eyes and take a look at his web design.

Eight Legs And Counting

These creepy-crawly spiders will help your youngsters get a leg up on counting skills. To prepare, make a desired number of spider bodies by hot-gluing together large- and medium-sized black pom-poms as shown. Glue two wiggle eyes onto the smaller pom-pom on each spider. For each spider body, cut four black pipe cleaners in half to make eight spider legs. Then place the spider bodies and legs in your math center. Invite each child who visits this center to add eight legs to each spider's body. Watch out, Miss Muffet!

Bat Cave

Set up a bat cave in your reading center to encourage learning about the habits and characteristics of bats. To create a cave, drape a large blanket over a low table. Equip the bat cave with flashlights and an assortment of bat picture books. If desired, make a tape recording of yourself reading facts about bats, and invite youngsters to listen to the tape as they browse through the bat books in the deep, dark cave.

Sand Spiders

Little ones will get all caught up in this spider-filled sand table! Bury an assortment of plastic or rubber spiders, plastic spider rings, and spider-shaped confetti in your sand table. Use black yarn to weave a spider's web around the entire sand table. Be sure to leave large gaps in the web so youngsters can reach through it to play in the sand. Then invite youngsters to sift or dig for spiders in the sand. After they capture a few spiders, help them attach the spiders to the web around the table. This is one webbed site youngsters will want to visit frequently!

Thanksgiving

"A-maize-ing" Prints

Invite youngsters to create a "corn-ucopia" of grainy prints at your art table. To prepare, cut an ear of husked corn into three pieces. Insert plastic corncob holders into the ends of the corn pieces. Pour a thin layer of red, yellow, and blue paint on separate Styrofoam® meat trays. Place the corn and paint in the art center along with a supply of large white construction paper. Invite each child to roll the corn in the paint, then onto a sheet of paper to make a print. If desired, laminate each print so each of your little pilgrims will have a personal placemat for a Thanksgiving feast.

Pumpkin-Pie Dough

Add a little spice to your sensory center with a batch of this spicy play dough. Bring in some pie tins and rolling pins, and invite youngsters to use the dough to make some homemade pies—just like Grandma's!

2 cups flour
1 cup salt
2 cups water
3 teaspoons pumpkin-pie spice

orange food coloring/paste
2 tablespoons vegetable oil
4 teaspoons cream of tartar

Combine ingredients in a large pot. Cook on low heat. Stir until a dough forms and pulls away from the sides of the pot. Remove the dough and cool.

Cornmeal To Feel

Invite little ones to the sensory center to get a feel for this cornmeal activity. To prepare, replace the sand in your sand table with cornmeal supplied by parents. Or place a large tub of cornmeal on a low table. Then equip the center with measuring cups, bowls, and spoons. Explain to students that a Wampanoag Indian named Squanto taught the Pilgrims how to plant corn. The Pilgrims used the corn to make corn bread, hoecakes, and Indian pudding. Invite youngsters to the sensory center to explore this grainy food source. After several days of free exploration, move the cornmeal from the sand table to the cooking center. In that center, use a new package of cornmeal to make corn muffins for snacktime. Use the cornmeal from the sensory center to make corn muffins to feed the birds.

Gourds And Potatoes And Pumpkins, Oh My!

Give your discovery center a seasonal twist with some traditional Thanksgiving foods. Display a variety of fresh gourds, regular and miniature ears of Indian corn, walnuts, minipumpkins, sweet potatoes, and squash. Cut open some of the gourds, potatoes, and squash, and crack open a couple of walnuts. Place the cut foods in a shallow tub to contain any possible mess, and keep a container of disposable wipes nearby for quick cleanups. Provide several magnifying glasses; then invite children in this center to examine the items—inside and out—using their senses of sight, touch, and smell.

Nuts!

Your youngsters will go nuts over this addition to your sensory center! Pour a bag of assorted mixed nuts (unshelled) into a large tub. Add tongs, ice-cube trays, and egg cartons. Encourage each child who visits this center to fill an ice-cube tray or egg carton by using the tongs to place a nut in each section of a carton or tray. Children may choose to sort the nuts by type or size as they work. After students enjoy sorting and placing the nuts, add a nutcracker to the center. Your little ones will crack up over this fun method of fine-motor practice!

Transportation

First-Class Flight

If your youngsters have been learning about air travel, this center idea is just the ticket! To begin, arrange chairs to represent the cabin and cockpit of an airplane. Lay a belt on each seat; then put a magazine under each passenger's seat. Provide a tray of plastic cups and play food for flight attendants to serve to the passengers. After the plane is prepared for takeoff, invite each child in a small group to select a role to assume, either as the pilot, a flight attendant, or a passenger. Then have youngsters board the plane. Encourage each child to act out the role he selected. Ladies and gentlemen, welcome aboard!

Seriation Station

Invite youngsters to chug on into this sorting-and-seriation station to reinforce color and sequencing skills. First duplicate ten copies of the train-car pattern on page 63. Color one train car blue, two red, three orange, and four black. Cut out and laminate each pattern; then put them in the math center. Invite your children to sort the train car cutouts by color. Next, have them line up each set of train-car colors to make separate trains. Finally, have students put the color trains in order from shortest to longest. Toot! Toot!

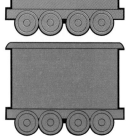

Transportation Mural

Put together sorting skills and art with this transportation mural. To begin, cut a six-foot length each of blue and green bulletin-board paper. Tape the lengths of paper together to represent an outdoor background with blue for the sky and green for the ground. Cut out a large lake shape from another piece of blue bulletin-board paper. Glue the lake cutout onto the outdoor background. Then cut out pictures of different kinds of vehicles from magazines and travel brochures. Place the background paper and the vehicle cutouts in a center along with glue, paintbrushes, and containers of black and white paint.

Encourage youngsters to visit this center and paint train tracks, roads, and clouds on the paper. After the paint dries, have them glue vehicle cutouts to the appropriate sections of the mural—such as boats on the lake, trains on the tracks, and planes in the sky. This depiction of trains, planes, and automobiles is sure to get two thumbs up!

The Wheels Go Round And Round

Transportation was changed forever when man discovered the wheel. Invite your little ones to make this discovery for themselves in your block center. Provide various types of building toys, such as LEGO® and DUPLO® blocks, but remove any wheels or wheeled pieces from the sets. Encourage youngsters in this center to build cars and trains. When they discover that they can't construct a vehicle that can move across the floor with a push, ask them what's missing. Then provide the wheels you've set aside and let them go ahead with their vehicle building. What *would* we do without wheels?

Transportation Tracks

Little ones will make tracks to the sand table for this activity. To prepare, add enough water to the sand so that it will remain wet for a long period of time. (Have a spray bottle of water on hand to wet the sand as needed.) Then place several toy vehicles with different wheel sizes in the sand table. Invite youngsters to drive the vehicles over the wet sand, leaving tire tracks; then have them park the vehicles near the sand table. Encourage the next group of visitors to match the vehicles to the corresponding tracks in the sand. To erase the tracks, have students smooth the sand with the palms of their hands. Time to start truckin' and trackin' all over again!

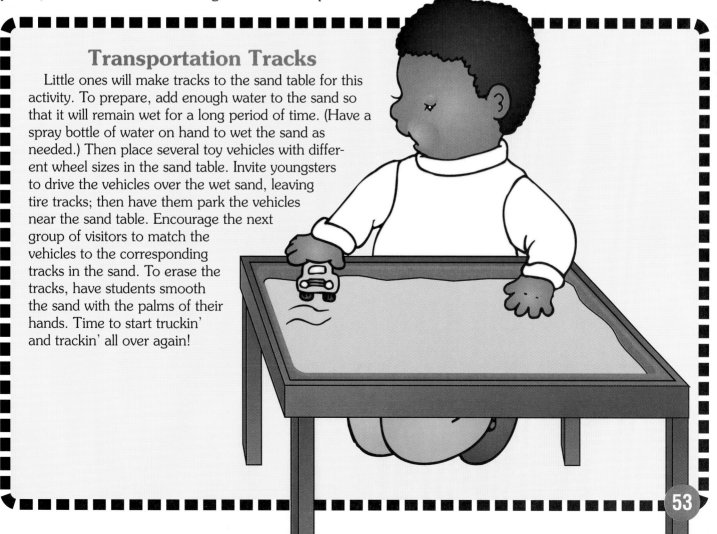

Valentine's Day

Wedding Bells

Valentine's Day is near and love is in the air! To celebrate, fill your dramatic-play center with all sorts of wedding clothes. Collect old suit jackets, formal dresses, scarves, high heels, plastic flower bouquets, and other wedding accessories. If desired, create a bridal veil from inexpensive netting and a child's headband. Then place the wedding attire in your center, along with a tape of the classic "Here Comes The Bride." Boys and girls alike will enjoy getting groomed during this month of love.

susan Hodnett

Sea Of Love

Zip up some learning about magnets with this discovery-center idea. To prepare, cut several heart shapes from sheets of craft foam or from brightly colored, plastic party cups. Attach a paper clip diagonally across each heart (to resemble an arrow). Place the clipped hearts into a quart-size zippered plastic bag; then partially fill the bag with red-tinted water. Carefully squeeze out any excess air; then seal the bag and add a strip of masking tape to prevent leaks. Make one or more of these bags as desired. Place the bag (or bags), along with a few magnets, in your discovery center. Invite youngsters to use the magnets to move the hearts through the water. Little ones will be attracted to this center!

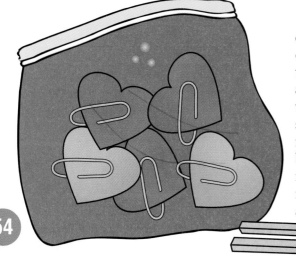

Valentines To Go

Invite youngsters to your art center to decorate these "heart-y" valentine-collection boxes. In advance, gather a class supply of cardboard laundry-detergent boxes with flip tops. Cover each box with white butcher paper. Put the covered boxes in your art center, along with a large supply of colored tissue-paper hearts, heart-shaped confetti, some paintbrushes, and a mixture of two parts glue and one part water.

At this center, invite each child to paint the glue mixture onto the sides and top of her box, then cover her box with tissue hearts and confetti. Allow time for the boxes to dry before attaching a ribbon handle to each one. Invite youngsters to use their boxes to collect valentine sweets and treats from their classmates during your Valentine's Day festivities.

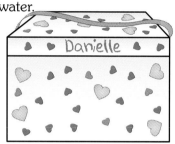

Candy Counting

Counting candy in the math center is sure to sweeten youngsters' skills with one-to-one correspondence. To prepare, gather several egg cartons. Cut one-cup to ten-cup segments from the cartons. Then place the egg-carton segments and a container of small candy hearts in the math center. Have each youngster select an egg-carton segment; then ask her to count the number of cups in the segment. Invite her to count out a corresponding number of candy hearts. Have her place one heart into each cup to check the accuracy of her counting. Then invite her to again count each sweet treat—as she pops them into her mouth to eat!

Patterns Of The Heart

Here's a "scent-sible" and seasonal way to practice patterning. To begin, make a batch of red, cherry-scented play dough. Then use large and small heart-shaped cookie cutters to trace repeating patterns onto a quantity of sentence strips. (Leave room on each strip so that youngsters can continue the pattern.) Laminate the pattern strips for durability. Then place the pattern strips, the cookie cutters, and the play dough in a center.

At this center, a child cuts large and small hearts from the play dough, then lays these hearts on a strip to extend the pattern.

Cherry Play Dough
2 1/2 cups flour
1 cup salt
1 tablespoon cream of tartar
2 packages unsweetened cherry Kool-Aid®
3 tablespoons cooking oil
2 cups boiling water

Mix the dry ingredients. Add the oil and boiling water. Stir quickly, mixing well. When cool, mix with your hands. Store in an airtight container.

FEEDING TIME

Invite youngsters to help the zookeeper feed the animals with this math-center activity. Prepare a simple bar graph by dividing a sheet of chart paper into five columns. Label each column with the name and picture of a different zoo animal. Make 15 construction-paper copies of the bucket pattern on page 63; then cut out and laminate the patterns. Tape-record yourself—the zookeeper—giving feeding instructions for each animal on the graph. For example, you might say, "Give the zebra one bucket of food" or "Give the elephant four buckets of food." Leave a long pause after each direction. Then record questions such as "Which animal has the most (or fewest) buckets of food?" or "How many more buckets of food does the [elephant] have than the [zebra]?"

Display the bar graph in your math center. Place the tape in a tape recorder, and arrange it, along with the feeding buckets and a supply of Sticky-Tac, in the center. Invite each child who visits this center to listen to the tape and attach the buckets to the graph as directed. Encourage youngsters to answer the questions at the end of the tape.

WHO BELONGS IN THE ZOO?

Which animals belong in the zoo? Use this block-center idea to see if your youngsters know. Place an assortment of toy animals in your block center, including zoo animals, farm animals, ocean animals, and house pets. Invite students to build zoo habitats with the blocks, adding rocks, green Easter grass, and plastic trees if they desire. Then ask students to separate the zoo animals from the other animals and place them in their new zoo homes. After they settle the zoo animals in, invite your little ones to line up the remaining animals for a tour of the zoo.

"PUZ-ZOO-ZLES"

Have youngsters practice sorting and sequencing skills as they assemble these puzzling zoo animals. Cut several large pictures of different zoo animals from nature magazines. Mount the pictures onto tagboard cards; then laminate the cards for durability. Cut each card into three vertical sections to create a simple animal puzzle. Then put all the puzzle pieces in a container.

To use this center, a child first sorts the pieces according to the puzzle to which they belong, then puts the strips in order to complete each animal "puz-zoo-zle."

SPOTS AND STRIPES

This activity will have your little artists spotting zoo animals of all kinds at your art center. Hang several pictures of spotted and striped zoo animals—such as zebras, tigers, giraffes, and leopards—in your art center. Set out zoo-animal stencils, markers, trays of paint, some round corks, and a few plastic hair combs.

Invite each youngster at this center to draw or trace a zoo animal. Have her dip a cork in paint to make spots on her animal. Or have her comb paint over her animal outline to give it stripes. After the paint dries, display these animals in a prominent place for all to spot!

GOIN' WILD

Youngsters will be wild about this dramatic-play center activity. To prepare, ask parents to donate old Halloween costumes of zoo animals (or items that can be used to create animal costumes) and pairs of old gloves. Hot-glue construction-paper claws to the gloves. If desired, make animal-ear headbands from sentence strips. Place the costume items in your dramatic-play center. Then invite visitors to this center to assemble their own zoo-animal costumes for some role-playing fun. Students will have a roaring good time!

57

Paper-Doll Pattern
Use with "Paper-Doll Pals"
on page 24.

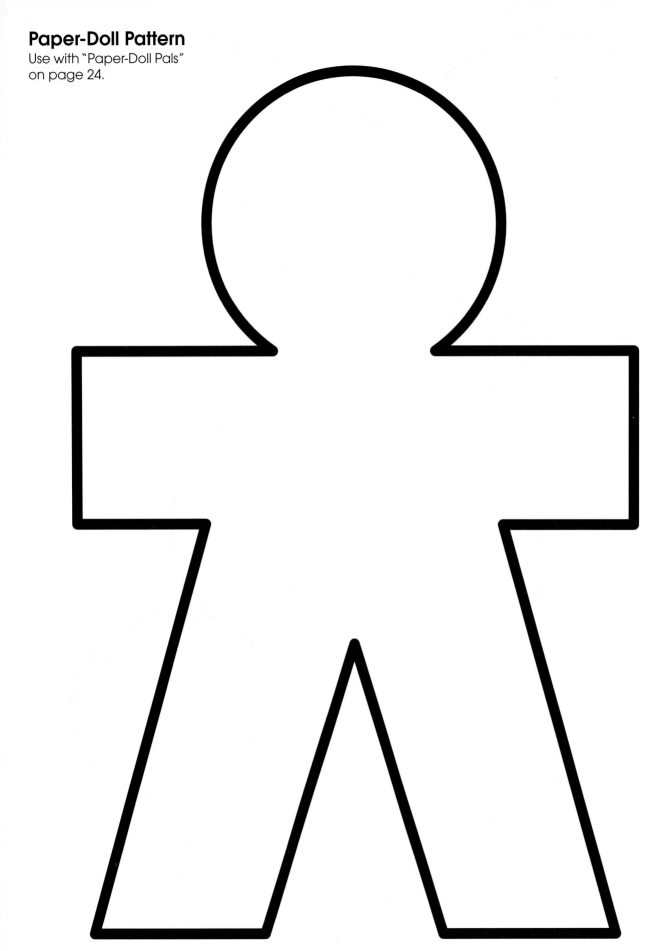

Safety Cards

Use with "Red Light, Green Light" on page 29.

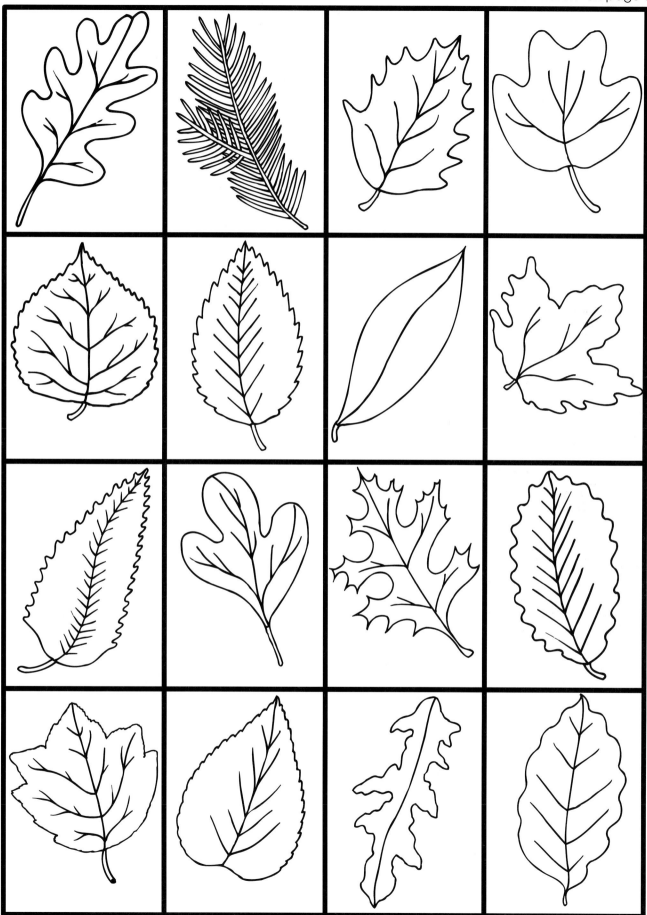

Sand-Pail And Fish Patterns

Use the sand-pail pattern with "Collecting Seashells" on page 38.
Use the fish pattern with "Oceans Of Bubbles" on page 39.

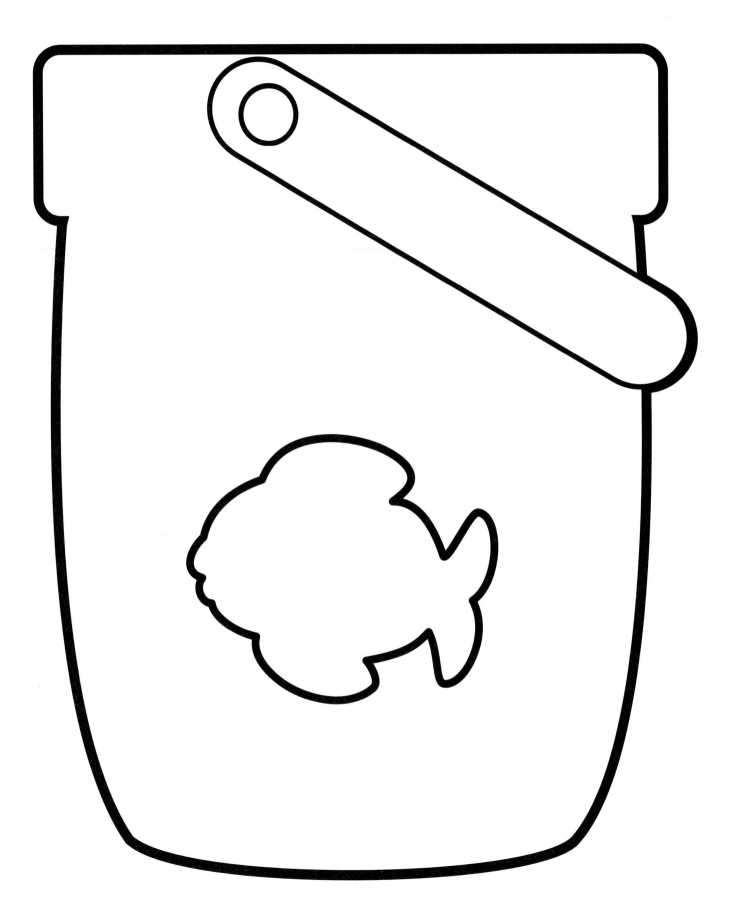

Train-Car Pattern
Use with "Seriation Station" on page 52.

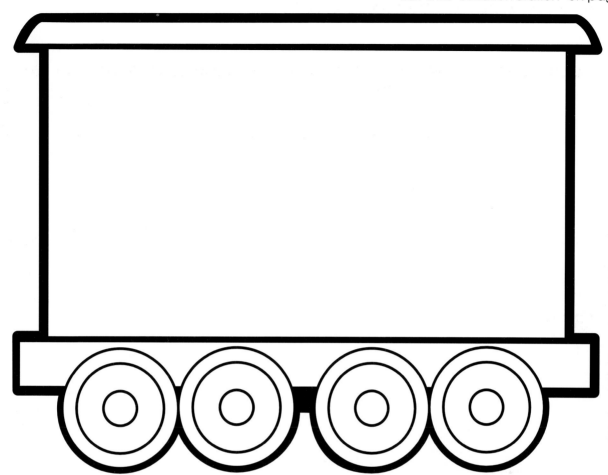

Bucket Pattern
Use with "Feeding Time" on page 56.

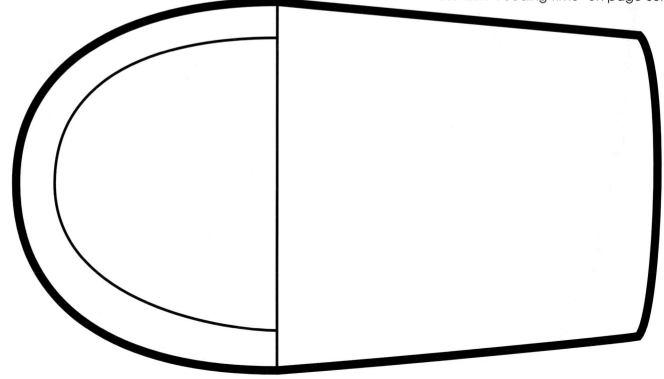

ABOUT THE AUTHORS

dayle timmons has been teaching "at-risk" preschoolers for eight years at the highly acclaimed Alimacani Elementary School, a national model school in Jacksonville, Florida. During her 25-year career in teaching special education, dayle has been named teacher-of-the-year in three different school districts. dayle enjoys sharing her ideas with other teachers and is a regular contributor to *The* Preschool *Mailbox®*. dayle lives in Jacksonville, Florida, with her husband, Jim, and two children. ▶

◀ **Jan Brennan** taught young children in a public school setting for seven years before deciding to home-school her own children, preschool through fourth grade. Jan contributes to *The* Preschool *Mailbox®* on a regular basis, currently by writing the feature "Building Bridges." Jan lives in Avon, Connecticut, with her husband, three sons, and a preschool-age daughter.

Lisa Leonardi has eight years of experience teaching full-day kindergarten and first grade. She is currently president of the Norfolk Cooperative Preschool and enjoys giving workshops and seminars for parents. Lisa has been sharing her ideas with teachers for three years as a freelance writer for The Education Center, Inc. Lisa lives in Norfolk, Massachusetts, with her husband and two daughters. ▶

◀ **Ann Flagg** has been working with young children in both public and private settings for 11 years. Ann taught preschool for five years and recently served as the director of Clarion Christian Preschool in Clarion, Pennsylvania. Writing for The Education Center, Inc., has been an ongoing part of Ann's contribution to the education of young children. Ann lives in Mesa, Arizona, with her husband and daughter.